# QUESTIONS AND ANSWERS
# ON COMMUNISM

# Questions and Answers

## on

## COMMUNISM

### Richard Cardinal Cushing

Third Printing

UT COGNOSCANT TE

ST. PAUL EDITIONS

Published by the DAUGHTERS OF ST. PAUL
*Jamaica Plain, Boston 30, Mass.*

# FOREWORD

*This booklet on Questions and Answers concerning Communism has been published with the hope that it might serve to arouse many from a state of apathy and indifference towards an international conspiracy that is bent on the domination of the world.*

*The questions are those most frequently asked in classrooms and lecture halls. The answers are taken mainly from Communist writings.*

*Papal encyclicals, reports of Congressional Committees and other sources of information, facts and guidance are quoted to substantiate our evaluation of the true and subtle nature of the enemy that confronts us.*

*This booklet, however, is by no means the complete picture of Communism nor a full answer to it. Whereas many would not read one or more of the innumerable volumes already written on the subject, they might study a summary of this type.*

*If they will, I pray that it may prompt them to live the way of life that is spelled out in the Gospels and the Ten Commandments. That way of life, for individuals and nations, is the first and greatest answer to the Communist peril. Thereafter every good reform needed in our country will follow and the roots of Communism in our midst will be destroyed.*

†Richard Cardinal Cushing

# TABLE OF CONTENTS

# CHAPTER I

# COMMUNISM, MARXISM, SOCIALISM

1. QUESTION: **What does Communism mean?**

   ANSWER: A. Literally it means the common ownership of all material goods: No private, individual ownership of wealth, property or productive goods.

   B. It is based on a world view called "dialectical materialism," which seeks to interpret the world as coming into being without God and to prove that He does not exist.

2. QUESTION: **How does Communism contend that it will "prove" that God does not exist?**

   ANSWER: A. By the assertion (which is only an assertion and which can readily be refuted) that matter is auto-dynamic or self-creating and

   B. By the promise (which is only a promise) of bringing about an earthly paradise, the so-called "Communist society."

3. QUESTION: **What will be the conditions of this "Communist society," according to the Communists?**

   ANSWER: It will be an era, they contend, where there will be no State, no family, and no morality of any sort. Man will be able in this condition, they foolishly assert, to end all unhappiness, neurosis, and ill health. Also, in that "Communist society," there will be "lasting peace" and "for the first time, genuine freedom."

4. QUESTION: **Are there any supposed stages in this achievement of the "Communist society?"**

ANSWER: Yes, the first stage is supposedly the achievement and consolidation of the world Soviet dictatorship or world socialism, which must be brought about in each country first by guile and then by violence. After this dictatorship has become world wide, the Communists contend it will actually "wither away" and in its place will come the promised earthly paradise or the Communist society.

5. QUESTION: **Have the Communists ever been able to answer the five proofs of St. Thomas Aquinas for the existence of God?**

ANSWER: No, they have always evaded the teachings of St. Thomas Aquinas.

6. QUESTION: **Is there actually any system of Communism anywhere?**

ANSWER: No. The word is a popular fraud. In Russia and in the other countries subject to Soviet rule, the leaders of the State control all wealth, property, and industry. They also, by that very fact, control the utterances and expressions of everyone, dominating every agency of public information.

7. QUESTION: **What does Communism (or its alleged current stage of socialism) actually mean?**

ANSWER: It means that all power, political, economic, social, and financial resides in the State, namely in the hands of the Soviet rulers.

8. QUESTION: **What is the proper name for this system?**

ANSWER: Marxism or Soviet Fascism, which means that all power is in the control of a few persons. It is extreme socialism which deifies Matter and the State. In its philosophy, the clod becomes God and man becomes a slave.

9. QUESTION: **What is Marxism?**

ANSWER: It is an alleged political-economic system (based on this world view of dialectical materialism or the denial of God) named after its founder, Karl Marx, born in Germany in 1818, died in England in 1883. He renounced both Judaism and Christianity in turn and became an avowed atheist. His principal works are **Das Kapital** and the **Communist Manifesto,** both written in collaboration with Frederick Engels.

10. QUESTION: **What was the background of Frederick Engels?**

ANSWER: Engels, who was born in 1820 and died in 1895, was the son of a wealthy textile manufacturer who had mills both in Germany and England. Engels not only wrote some of the most important Marxist works but also contributed financially to Marx' support.

11. QUESTION: **What is the theme or message of the two chief Marxist works?**

ANSWER: A. **Das Kapital,** called the bible of Marxism, the first volume of which was completed in 1867, is a long, complicated treatise in three volumes on the history of the class struggle through the ages, allegedly culminated in class warfare between the workers and their oppressors, namely the capitalists or the employing class. It contains the philosophy of Marx (Dialectic Materialism), his economic theories, and his proposed methods of removing most economic and social evils.

B. **The Communist Manifesto,** 1848, outlines the strategy for all workers of the world in overthrowing the hated system of Capitalism: to take wealth and industry from the middle and upper classes (Bourgeoisie) and allegedly transfer them to the workers, i.e., the Proletariat. (Actually, by standing for "the dictatorship of the proletariat," which is in reality the dictatorship over the proletariat, Marx and his successors prevented or tried to prevent that wider diffusion of property which is essential to social progress and justice.)

12. QUESTION: **Did Marx and Engels write other books besides these two chief ones?**

ANSWER: Yes, they produced a great number of works, from **The Holy Family,** written before the **Communist Manifesto** all the way over to **Ludwig Feuerbach** and the **Dialectics of Nature,** written by Frederick Engels after Marx' death. Each one of these books seeks to denounce the existence of God and the value of religion as the basis for all Marxist teachings.

13. QUESTION: **Why is the basic teaching of Marx called Dialectical Materialism?**

ANSWER: A. Materialism denies the existence of any non-material reality such as God, the soul, and the world of the spirit. "The only reality is matter" is a constant Communist refrain. Marx used the scientific fact that the matter of the universe is in constant motion, often evolving into new forms of mineral, plant, and organic life to prove that this also applies to the basic creation of life and the origin of the human mind. How life and reason ever developed from atoms and molecules of mere matter Marx does not and cannot explain. Nor can he tell us how the motion which he makes so much of can come into existence without a First Mover, namely, Almighty God.

B. The Dialectic according to Marx is the logic or "method" of his theory of materialism. It supposedly rules the inevitable laws of nature, society, and right thinking. It is based on the false assumption that every idea (and every development in nature and history) contains within itself its opposite or denial. This is called the operation of Thesis, Anti-thesis, and Synthesis. For instance, in our present period of history, the Communists contend that the thesis (or ruling class or "thing that is") is the so-called bourgeoisie; the antithesis is the proletariat; and the synthesis is the dictatorship of the proletariat or socialism, the first stage of Communism.

Actually, we have seen that this alleged dictatorship of the proletariat is nothing other than the dictatorship of the Communist Party. This fact is acknowledged by both Lenin and Stalin, the latter in his famous **Problems of Leninism.**

14. QUESTION: **What is the name given by the Communists to the alleged operation of the "laws" of dialectical materialism in society?**

ANSWER: It is called by the Communists "historical materialism," which Frederick Engels claims is one of the great "discoveries" of Karl Marx.

15. QUESTION: **What are some of the errors in the theories of Karl Marx?**

ANSWER: A. His false basic assertion that God does not exist and that the universe has come into being without God. From this all the other errors of Marxism flow.

B. His equally false statement that history is entirely determined by economic factors. As with all errors that try to win man's acceptance, this is partially true. But the great religious, judicial, and other "idealistic" developments in world history did not arise from economic influences. It could be shown that even Marx' own teaching begins as something which arises from the process of thought, that is, not the outcome of material or economic forces.

C. Marx and Engels regarded private ownership of property as essentially evil. It is the abuse or misuse of private property which is evil. What the Marxist view of private property will finally lead to in the destruction of the family is testified to by Engels in his famous work, **The Origin of the Family, Private Property, and the State.**

D. The labor involved in producing any material commodity is not the principal factor in its value, as Marx claimed. Skill, demand and supply, climate, weather, etc., are important factors of value.

16. QUESTION: **What are some important truths in the writings of Marx?**

ANSWER: A. The fact that millions of workers in Europe, England, America and elsewhere were underpaid, or unemployed.

B. The fact that Economic Liberalism (irresponsible use of capital) was a common cause of this condition.

C. The deplorable conditions of child-labor in the 19th century.

Note: Marx failed to realize that Socialism would lead, as it has, to worse exploitation of the workers than the system of Private Enterprise. Marxism-Leninism as a whole, in attacking the undoubted abuses of "monopoly" in the capitalist system, could only offer as their solution a still greater monopoly in dictatorship of a Party and hence of a very few through the State apparatus. This led to the monopoly not only of property but also of the press, all other avenues of information, and hence, the control of thinking.

17. QUESTION: **Why is Marxism today called "Marxism-Leninism" by the Communists?**

ANSWER: Because the teachings of Marx and Engels were later supplemented by those of V. I.

Lenin, who re-affirmed strongly the basic materialism of Marxism and in addition the necessity under the Marxist theory for the final violent overthrow of all non-socialist governments. This necessity, he averred, applied also to the governments of the United States and Great Britain, which must "inevitably" be overthrown by violence in order to introduce socialism.

As Joseph V. Stalin puts it in his **Foundations of Leninism:** Leninism is Marxism of the era "of the proletarian revolution". To which he adds: "To be more exact, Leninism is the theory and tactics of the proletarian revolution in general, the theory and tactics of the dictatorship of the proletariat in particular."

18. QUESTION: **What are the "Marxist-Leninist classics" to which the Communists always refer in their writings?**

ANSWER: They are the teachings and therefore the works of "the great scientists of Marxism-Leninism," namely, Karl Marx, Frederick Engels, V. I. Lenin, Joseph V. Stalin, Mao Tse-tung, and today Nikita Khrushchev.

19. QUESTION: **Does the Catholic Church condemn Socialism in theory and practice?**

ANSWER: Several recent popes, especially Leo XIII and Pius XI, have frequently stated that Socialism in any form is wrong. Strict Socialism puts all productive goods under the ownership and control of the State contrary to the individual right of ownership. The control of Education, and of every other social institution, is a natural consequence. What is popularly called "Limited Social- ism," such as State or Federal control of Railroads or Communications, may be nec- essary in the interest of the common good. However, "the Limited Socialist experi- ments" in England, for example, have done little to improve social and economic con- ditions.

20. QUESTION: **What three things should be borne con- stantly in mind in connection with Soviet Communism?**

ANSWER: These three things are:

A. The nature of Communism, flowing from its world outlook of dialectical material- ism and therefore the "necessity" of set- ting up the world Soviet dictatorship first by guile and then by violence, in order to usher in the "earthly paradise" of the Communist society.

B. The nature of the Communist line and the methods by which it is introduced by infiltration into every non-Socialist coun- try. The Communist line is that series of proposals which Moscow initiates and then wants the so-called "free world" to adopt in order to bring about the weak- ening of non-Socialist countries so that they may be eventually destroyed.

C. The true Communist attitude toward re- forms. By this we will know that reforms are used by the Communists merely as a "screen or cover" for their illegal activi- ties to bring about the dictatorship. This is what Stalin tells us in his section on "Revolutionism and Reformism" in his **Foundations of Leninism.**

## REFERENCES AND SUGGESTED READINGS:

1. Budenz, Louis F. **Men Without Faces.** New York: Harper and Brothers.
2. Budenz, Louis F. **Techniques of Communism.** Chicago: Henry Regnery.
3. R. N. Carew Hunt. **Theory and Practice of Communism.** New York: Macmillan.
4. Gitlow, Benjamin. **The Whole of Their Lives.** New York: Scribner and Co.
5. Hoover, J. Edgar. **Masters of Deceit.** New York: Henry Holt and Co.
6. Kravchenko, Victor. **I Chose Freedom.** New York: Scribner and Co.
7. The Rev. Charles A. McFadden. **Philosophy of Communism.** New York: Benziger Brothers.
8. Pius XI. **Encyclical on Atheistic Communism,** March 19, 1937.
9. Sheen, Bishop Fulton J. **Communism and the Conscience of the West.** Bobbs and Merrill, Pub.

# CHAPTER II

# THE NATURE OF COMMUNISM

1. QUESTION: **What does Pope Pius XI declare to be the first or basic cause for the rapid spread of Communism?**

   ANSWER: In the middle of his Encyclical, **Divini Redemptoris,** (on Atheistic Communism) Pope Pius XI asks the question: "How is it possible that such a system, long since rejected scientifically and now proved erroneous by experience, how is it, We ask, that such a system could spread so rapidly in all parts of the world?"

   And he answers: "The explanation lies in the fact that too few have been able to grasp the nature of Communism."

2. QUESTION: **What, then, is the nature of Communism?**

   ANSWER: As we have seen, Communism is not so much a social or economic theory, as most people suppose, although certain outstanding social and economic theories flow from its original premise. It is rather a world outlook, an alleged explanation of how the world began automatically and how it will "inevitably" go forward in the history of man.

3. QUESTION: **Is there strong proof in the Marxist-Leninist "classics" and in the continuing Communist**

comments on them that dialectical materialism is the world outlook of the Communists?

ANSWER:     Most decidedly. This conception saturates all
the "classics" and for Marx and Engels is
summed up in Engels' noteworthy work,
**Ludwig Feuerbach.** This work, completed
in 1888, not only seeks to summarize and
pronounce "dialectical materialism" as the
world outlook of the Communists, but seeks
to go on to show that this viewpoint does
not permit the least thought of any "reality"
but matter. It is stark, naked materialism.

V. I. Lenin continued and expanded on the
emphasis of dialectical materialism as the
Communist world view in the whole of
volume XI of his **Selected Works.** Stalin
summed up the whole assertion when he
wrote: "Dialectical materialism is the world
outlook of the Marxist-Leninist party. It is
called dialectical materialism because its ap-
proach to the phenomena of nature, its
method of studying and apprehending them,
is **dialectical,** while its interpretation of the
phenomena of nature, its conception of these
phenomena, its theory, is **materialistic.**"

4. QUESTION:   **Do the Communists consider this affirmation
of this world outlook to be important?**

ANSWER:     They have considered this basic thought of
so much importance that they have reprint-
ed the statements by all "the great Marxist
scientists" in this regard over and over
again, in many different forms. It is the trag-
edy of America and most Americans, including many of our leaders, that this huge
distribution of Marxist-Leninist fundamental

literature goes on without their knowing anything about it.

As an illustration, chapter no. 4 of his **History of the Communist Party of the Soviet Union,** in which Stalin makes his statement on dialectical materialism and then explains it at length, is distributed by the thousands of copies as a pamphlet entitled **Dialectical and Historical Materialism.**

5. QUESTION: **Has any recent Communist declaration re-asserted this basic foundation of dialectical materialism?**

   ANSWER: The Program of the Communist International, adopted by the Sixth World Communist Congress in Moscow in 1928, sums up its beliefs by beginning with the phrase: "Advocating and propagating the dialectical materialism of Marx and Engels and employing it as a revolutionary method of conceiving reality. . ." From thence it goes on through the entire range of resulting Communist beliefs to the logical declaration that it (the Communist International) "openly comes out as the organizer of the International Proletarian Revolution."

   The famous Declaration of Communist and Workers Parties of Socialist Countries, issued in Moscow in November, 1957, asserts: "The theory of Marxism-Leninism derives from dialectical materialism. This world outlook reflects the universal law of development of nature, society and human thinking. It is valid for the past, the present and the future."

6. QUESTION: **Do we have additional proof in the writings of Communist scholars that dialectical ma-**

terialism is the all-embracing world outlook upon which all their other views are based?

ANSWER: Yes, we have it in the writings of every Communist theoretician. As an illustration, Maurice Cornforth, the British Communist scholar, in his work, **Materialism and the Dialectic Method,** says definitely that the theory on which the Communist Party establishes all its theories and policies "is the theory of Marxism-Leninism." Then he says: "And it is not just an economic theory, not yet exclusively a political theory, but a world outlook—a philosophy."

7. QUESTION: **How do the "laws" of dialectical materialism operate in nature, according to the Communists?**

ANSWER: Matter and motion have always been inseparable, they contend. This motion, producing different stages in the development of nature and mankind, is always a motion of conflict or debate, dialectical motion.

8. QUESTION: **What is the fundamental and devastating weakness of this theory right in the beginning?**

ANSWER: Its weakness is—and from this it never recovers—that neither Marx nor Engels nor any of their followers can explain from where this alleged motion comes. They cannot answer the argument of St. Thomas Aquinas that the existence of motion in matter proves the existence of the First Mover, Almighty God. Engels admits that the Communists do not know the origin of this alleged motion, expressing the hope that in time science will be able to show how it develops.

9. QUESTION: **Despite this flimsy and false foundation, how do the Communists proceed to explain the workings of dialectical materialism in nature?**

ANSWER: Their contention is that the motion in what we consider to be inert matter (the original matter of the world) caused that which was at that time (thesis) to be challenged by the new form of life that was to be (anti-thesis) and out of this conflict came a new stage (synthesis). In this way, in these first stages, there developed life, then after millions of years, higher forms of animal existence, then after more millions of years there came into being man himself.

10. QUESTION: **Do the Communists try to present in detail the course of this dialectical conflict or motion in nature?**

ANSWER: Yes. They assert that in the course of this motion or struggle, there first begins to develop what they call a **quantitative** change, which after a time brings about a great and violent leap. Through that process, there comes about a **qualitative** change, namely, a new stage in nature.

11. QUESTION: **What are the five arguments for the existence of God given by St. Thomas Aquinas which the Communists evade in this alleged theory of dialectical materialism?**

ANSWER: The five arguments for the existence of God, which the Communists cannot answer are:
a) The existence of motion in matter proves

the existence of a First Mover, moved by no other, and that is God.

b) In the world of sensible things, there is an order of efficient causes, but there is no cause known which is found to be an efficient cause in itself. Therefore, it is necessary to admit a first efficient cause, God.

c) In nature, everything that we observe has a possibility to be and not to be, becoming generated and then corrupted. This makes it necessary for a force which has an existence of its own, called God.

d) There is a gradation to be found in things regarding their goodness and the like. There must be therefore something which is to all beings, the cause of their being, goodness and every other perfection. That is God.

e) The design existing in the universe, whereby natural bodies which lack knowledge nevertheless act for an end, indicates that there is some intelligent being by whom all natural things are directed. That is God.

12. QUESTION: **Is the dialectical materialism of the Communists, then, any different from the mechanistic materialism of the 18th Century?**

ANSWER: No, since the Communists are unable to prove whence their alleged motion comes, they are in no better way than the old materialists who found themselves in difficulty because they could not show how mankind or the world could come into being without God.

The alleged "law of opposites," whereby the Communists contend that every existing thing or being has within it a "unity of opposites," which sets it into motion, is totally unproved.

13. QUESTION: **Nevertheless, Marxism-Leninism goes on, does it not, to assert that this dialectic motion also exists in society through what is known as historical materialism?**

ANSWER: That is correct. It asserts that accordingly there was originally primitive Communism, then the slave state, then feudalism, capitalism, and inevitably after that, socialism, or the dictatorship of the proletariat.

14. QUESTION: **Is there a fundamental defect in this interpretation of history?**

ANSWER: There are many defects, which we shall have to examine later. One of these is that the claims that economic conditions determine the morals, religion, and law of each period is not true. The Catholic Church has existed through the slave state, feudalism, and capitalism.

Another defect of this theory is that it cannot account for periods of retrogression in history.

15. QUESTION: **How is it, according to the Communists, that the world Soviet dictatorship will "wither away" into the perfect Communist society and thus end the dialectical process in history?**

ANSWER: They base this theory on a false understanding of the nature of the state, as we shall see when we come to that subject. But they assert that this earthly paradise will come about as though it were an unanswerable truth. At the 21st Congress of the Communist Party of the Soviet Union, Nikita Khrushchev even announced that the beginnings of this Communist society will open up in Soviet Russia and the captive nations at the end of the next seven years.

16. QUESTION: **According to Marxism-Leninism, what is necessary to bring in this earthly paradise of the Communist society?**

ANSWER: It is necessary that the Soviet dictatorship, or socialism, shall become world-wide—established, maintained, and consolidated on a world scale. Or, at least, that the capitalist (or free) world shall become so encircled and weakened that the world-wide character of the dictatorship will be assured.

Then, the dictatorship will supposedly wither away of its own volition, yielding its place to the Communist society without state, law, family, morality, church. At the same time, it will supposedly end all unhappiness and ill health.

17. QUESTION: **What practical problem does this determination of the Communists to build the world Soviet dictatorship, in order to bring about the earthly paradise, present to the United States and the other free nations of the world?**

ANSWER: It presents them with the cold, hard fact that they cannot deal with Soviet Russia or with the international Communist conspiracy by way of negotiations, without bringing about defeat of the free world. The Communists will use every method—negotiations, civil war, as in the Baltic countries, Korean wars, and thrusts against us as in the Middle East and Asia—in order to obtain the world Soviet dictatorship.

18. QUESTION: **Does the record of Soviet Russia regarding treaties bear out this conclusion?**

ANSWER: Yes. Studies of the Senate Sub-Committee on Internal Security of the United States show that Soviet Russia has broken fifty of the fifty-two treaties it has signed.

## REFERENCES AND SUGGESTED READINGS:

1. Special study is suggested of **The Philosophy of Communism,** by the Reverend Charles J. McFadden, OSA.
2. **Basic Writings of St. Thomas Aquinas,** edited by Anton G. Pegis. Vol. I., Random House, New York.
   (A brief critical analysis of some of the Communist writings referred to in this and other chapters will be found at the end of this booklet.)

CHAPTER III

# CLASS WAR AND
# THE COMMUNIST LINE

1. QUESTION: **According to Marxism-Leninism, what is the dynamic force which brings about the dialectical motion in society—the carrying forward of thesis, antithesis, and synthesis?**

   ANSWER: It is the class war, sometimes also called the class struggle. Marx and Engels stressed this idea definitely in the **Communist Manifesto,** when they said: "The whole history of mankind ... has been a history of class struggles, conflicts between exploiting and exploited, ruling and oppressed classes."

2. QUESTION: **Did Pope Pius XI also warn us of the class war theory of the Communists?**

   ANSWER: Yes. In the noted Encyclical on Atheistic Communism, His Holiness refers to the "trickery" of the Communists, giving as one example the following: "Thus, aware of the universal desire for peace, the leaders of Communism pretend to be the most zealous promoters and propagandists in the movement for world amity. Yet, at the same time, they stir up a class warfare which causes rivers of blood to flow."

   Then the Pope added: "And realizing that their system offers no internal guarantee of peace, they have recourse to unlimited armaments."

3. QUESTION: **Did the Communist Manifesto develop this idea of the class war to make it a universal phenomenon of all history?**

   ANSWER: It did. And so we read: "The history of all hitherto existing society is the history of class struggles. Freeman and slave, patrician and plebian, lord and serf, guild-master and journeyman, in a word, oppressor and oppressed stood in constant opposition to one another, carried on an uninterrupted now hidden, now open fight, a fight that each time ended, either in a revolutionary reconstitution of society at large, or in the common ruin of the contending classes."

4. QUESTION: **Is this theory of the class war based on valid grounds in history?**

   ANSWER: No. Like practically all Marxist concepts, it is an over-simplification of the facts, a fitting of the facts into a preconceived idea.

5. QUESTION: **In what way is the Marxian theory of the class war an over-simplification?**

   ANSWER: In countless ways. Historians and philosophers have pointed out that this theory, making all history the result of a dialectical process inevitably followed through and operating solely by means of economic motives, pressures, and conflicts, fails to take into consideration a thousand cross-currents that characterize history.

6. QUESTION: **This false theory of the class struggle is bound up, then, in the idea of economic determinism in history?**

   ANSWER: Yes. The basic idea of Marx (since there are no actual spiritual forces except those that arise from materialistic conditions) is that the driving force of the class struggle comes from economic conflict. That idea, in turn, is taken from the false conception that all religion, law, and other spiritual developments of an epoch in history are actually the outcome of the mode of production and distribution of food, clothing, and shelter.

7. QUESTION: **Does the history of Communism itself disprove this materialistic conception of history?**

ANSWER: It emphatically does. Christopher Dawson has pointed out in his **Essays in Order** that Marxism-Leninism had its origin in the mind of "that arch-individualist, Karl Marx, and the forces that inspired him were neither of the economic or of the material order."

8. QUESTION: **Do we see this theory of the class war disproved in our own day?**

ANSWER: Of course we do. The alleged victory for the working class in Soviet Russia and in other Soviet-controlled countries is actually a victory for the dictatorship of the Communist Party, itself under control of an oligarchy ruled by one dictator. The present personal dictator of the whole Soviet domain is Nikita Khrushchev.

9. QUESTION: **In addition, wherein again does this theory of the class war carried by means of the dialectical method prove to be false?**

ANSWER: In the static character which is given to it in the future. The dialectical process, represented in history by the conflict of classes, is supposed to come to a complete halt when the world Soviet dictatorship has ushered in the Communist society or earthly paradise.

10. QUESTION: **Is the theory of the class war, although false, of serious concern to us today?**

ANSWER: It decidedly is; for the Communists contend that this "class war" has now developed into the international arena. It is being fought out primarily between the greatest "bourgeois" state, the United States of America, and the "camp of socialism, peace, and democracy," Soviet Russia. As we shall see later, under the Marxist ethic or Leninist morality, the Communists will use any means, fair or foul, to bring about the destruction of the United States in this "class war."

11. QUESTION: **In the present "class war." do the Communists hold that there must be violence at every step of the Red techniques in defeating the enemy?**

ANSWER: No, although the final achievement of the "dictatorship of the proletariat," which is the consummation of the "class war," must come about through violence.

12. QUESTION: **This means, does it not, that the historical and successful carrying forward of the "class war" in the United States must result in the violent overthrow of our government?**

ANSWER: That is correct. Stalin put it well for the Communists in his guide book, **The Foundations of Leninism,** when he wrote: "The dictatorship of the proletariat cannot arise as the result of the peaceful development of bourgeois society and of bourgeois democracy; it can arise only as the result of the

2

> smashing of the bourgeois state machine, the bourgeois army, the bourgeois bureaucratic machine, the bourgeois police."

13. QUESTION: **Does this violent "smashing" of the governmental machine apply to the United States?**

ANSWER: Yes. It emphatically applies to the government of the United States which from the Communist viewpoint must be overthrown by violence. Both Lenin in **State and Revolution** and Stalin in **The Foundations of Leninism** have stated specifically that the Government of the United States must be overthrown by violence, in order to achieve the Communist goal of the "proletarian dictatorship."

14. QUESTION: **But it has been said that every step in the class war is not necessarily to be pursued by violence?**

ANSWER: Of course not. The Communists must first undermine the governments of "bourgeois" states by getting them to follow the Communist line and thus persuade them to undermine their own strength.

15. QUESTION: **What is the Communist line?**

ANSWER: The Communist line is that series of proposals which Moscow wants free world countries to adopt at any particular period in order that those countries will weaken themselves by thus doing what Moscow wants them to do.

16. QUESTION: **How is the Communist line carried forward in any particular non-Soviet country?**

ANSWER: As Stalin has so clearly set down in his **Foundations of Leninism,** the Communist

Party in each country is to forward the Communist line by means of non-Communists and "non-party organizations," making of them "transmission belts" for this Communist line.

17. QUESTION: **The Communist line is often carried forward in any particular country, then, by non-Communists?**

ANSWER: Yes, that is its particular strength. Concealed Communists, following the directives given by Moscow, whether in Government, press, television, or anywhere else, pursuade leading non-Communists of the value of the line.

18. QUESTION: **Has the line been prevalent in decisions in the United States, in the attitude of our Government, the press, and the like?**

ANSWER: It has been the secret of Soviet success in the United States, persuading first our press and our other sources of information in large part, to spread it through America, and then getting certain leading officials in the Government to follow Moscow's directives.

19. QUESTION: **Has this been an effective method to influence the United States to help build up Soviet Power throughout the world?**

ANSWER: It has been the decisive means by which Moscow has induced the United States during the past twenty-five years—sometimes with hesitation, but always too frequently—to build up Soviet Power. It can be said that none of the nations now behind the Iron Curtain (known as captive nations) would be enslaved by the Soviet dictatorship today were it not for the aid given that dictatorship by our Government and our sources of information.

20. QUESTION: **When we say this, do we mean that every American official and every American source of information thus follow the Communist line?**

ANSWER: Certainly not. There are some officials and some sources of information that were intelligent enough and alert enough to oppose the line. But by and large, the line was far too successful in bringing about the great retreats and defeats for the United States during the past twenty-five years.

21. QUESTION: **Can you give a striking example of the victory of the Communist line by consent of the United States Government?**

ANSWER: Of the many that could be cited, the one that first comes to mind is the recognition of Soviet Russia by the United States in 1933. This gave to atheistic Communism and its representatives a prestige on which they built their continued conquest of great sections of the globe.

22. QUESTION: **At this time, were we given examples of Soviet perfidy in connection with our Government's agreeing to follow the Communist line?**

ANSWER: We were indeed: a perfidy which has distinguished all Soviet acts. For one thing, in the Roosevelt-Litvinov Pact of recognition, Soviet Russia agreed solemnly and in writing to end all subversive activities in the United States. This, of course, turned out to be a farce, since the Communist Party of the United States appeared in 1935 at the Seventh World Congress of the Communist International and joined with the other parties in acclaiming Stalin as "the leader, teacher, and guide of the proletariat and oppressed of the whole world."

23. QUESTION: **Were there any other Communist acts at this time which showed the dishonest character of this agreement on the part of the Kremlin?**

ANSWER: Most decidedly. Several months before the Roosevelt-Litvinov agreement was signed, the Communist Party here had received instructions from Moscow to Sergei I. Gussev, who had operated here as Communist International representative under the name of P. Green. This directive from Moscow led to the famous "Open Letter to the Party," ordering infiltration into every area of American life. It was then that infiltration began on a large scale in the Government (this being the time when Alger Hiss and his co-conspirators of the Washington "cell" entered the Government).

24. QUESTION: **Was there any other feature of this Roosevelt-Litvinov agreement which showed that Soviet Russia could not be trusted at any time?**

ANSWER: There was indeed. For as was to be the case right along in Soviet-American relations, the Kremlin was to persuade us that everything it wanted us to do was in order to obtain "peace." That is what President Roosevelt and "President" Kalinin declared in exchanging notes agreeing to the act of recognition. At that very time, both **Inprecor (International Press Correspondence,** the Communist International reportorial agency at that time for the comrades) and the **Daily Worker** in this country declared that real peace could never come except by the overthrow of the capitalist system and those countries which supported it.

25. QUESTION: **How does the Communist line come to this country?**

ANSWER: a) By the Communist International representative, who functions in the shadow of the United States, directing the Communist Party here from Moscow. b) By means of the publications sent throughout the world from Moscow (and now Peking) and by their echoes in the United States, designed for American Communist consumption.

26. QUESTION: **Were the names of the Communist International Representatives known in the past to the Government of the United States?**

ANSWER: They have not only come to be known, but the list of them down to Gerhart Eisler and J. Peters, the latter of whom instructed Whittaker Chambers in espionage in Washington, have been published by the Senate Sub-Committee on Internal Security. These names can be obtained from the Research Department of that Senate Sub-Committee.

27. QUESTION: **Are the publications which convey the line from Moscow and Peking known, and can they be readily obtained?**

ANSWER: They are well known, and can be obtained in English editions in at least three main Communist book stores in mid-Manhattan, New York.

28. QUESTION: **What are these publications?**

ANSWER: At this period they are: **The World Marxist Review,** which goes into 83 countries in their respective tongues each month and is the chief directive-giver. **International Affairs** and **New Times,** going regularly to the 83 countries from Moscow itself. And then, in the United States, **Political Affairs,** the official theoretical organ of the Party and formerly known as the **The Communist,** and **The Worker,** which is the telegraph agency of the conspiracy to its active followers.

29. QUESTION: **How does the Communist line originate, in order that it be carried forward by these publications?**

ANSWER: It originates in the "report" of the dictator of Soviet Russia, who is also the leader of world Communism, to the various "congresses" of the Communist Party of the Soviet Union. Today the line throughout the world is based on the "report" of Dictator Nikita Khrushchev to the 20th and 21st Congresses of the Communist Party of the Soviet Union. The first of these was held in February, 1956, and the second in January, 1959.

30. QUESTION: **What are the main features of the current Communist line?**

ANSWER: a) "Face to face meetings between the leaders of the East and West," in order that thereby the United States will be pledged in world opinion to acquiescence in the enslavement of the peoples behind the Iron Curtain. This had been achieved in the visit of Dictator Khrushchev to the United States, by which in effect we put our sanction on the slaughter of the Hungarians and the tyranny over the captive nations. At least that was the impression made by the visit on people from behind the Iron Curtain.

b) "Cultural exchanges," a big feature of the February, 1956 "report" by Dictator Khrushchev. This is designed to expand the Soviet espionage—military, political, and industrial—which formerly produced such servants of the Kremlin as Alger Hiss in the Government and the Rosenbergs. This process is now going forward, and the United States is now wide open to Soviet espionage against our country.

c) The final breaking down of all security precautions in the United States against the Communist conspiracy, by making permanent the American superstition engendered by the Reds in "the battle against McCarthyism." This has now gone so far as the result of the Supreme Court decisions, which have been criticized by the American Bar Association, that the United States is now without internal security protection of any real kind.

d) Persuading the United States to go to a "Summit meeting," which has been a big item in the current Communist line. It is designed to achieve at least two purposes: 1) to attain new Communist conquest in Asia,

Africa, or Latin America while the United States is distracted by long talks which come to no agreement, and 2) to create serious rifts among the Western Powers, particularly possible since Great Britain seems constantly given to the appeasement tendency.

e) To get the United States eventually to make such concessions on West Berlin and West Germany as to make certain the final achievement of a Soviet Germany and therefore of a Soviet Europe.

f) To persuade the United States to agree to the recognition of Red China and to the admission of that barbarous regime into the United Nations, in order to make easier the Communist conquest of all Asia and also Red dominance in Latin America, where the "prestige" of Red China is being used in Moscow's infiltration.

g) Strengthening of the Communist Party in this country by complete failure to do anything substantial against that conspiracy and by the encouragement to appeasement raised by the Khrushchev visit. This is to be accompanied by a great campaign for the infiltration of the youth of the nation, first by getting them to adopt features of the Communist line and then by getting key figures among the young people to become secret Marxists.

31. QUESTION: **Is it possible to know and thereby combat the Communist line?**

ANSWER: Most decidedly. That is our main current responsibility. It can be done by following the

pamphlets and articles that we and others
write, by learning each week from the col-
umn by Louis F. Budenz, "The Reds, What
Now?" appearing in many Catholic news-
papers and by reading articles and books
prepared by authorities who know from
study and experience the policies and pro-
grams of Communism.

# CHAPTER IV

# THE COMMUNIST ATTITUDE
# TOWARD REFORMS

1. QUESTION: **Do the Communists claim to be fervid champions of reforms?**

   ANSWER: Most decidedly. They claim constantly, in almost a chant, that they are in the "forefront" of the battle for the trade unions, in the struggle for the colonial peoples, and for Negro rights, and against anti-Semitism.

2. QUESTION: **Why, then, do the Communists constantly condemn the "reformists"?**

   ANSWER: Because the reformists actually believe in the reforms they advocate, whereas Communists advance reforms only in order to forward the Communist line and then to bring about the dictatorship.

3. QUESTION: **Has Pope Pius XI specifically called our attention to the hypocritical use by the Communists of reforms for their own subversive purposes?**

   ANSWER: Yes, His Holiness has done so in a number of places in his Encyclical on **Atheistic Communism,** warning us to cultivate "distrust of Communist tactics." In one sentence on this subject, he says: "Without receding an inch from their subversive principles, they invite Catholics to collaborate with them in the realm of so-called humanitarianism and charity; and at times even make proposals that are in perfect harmony with the Christian spirit and the doctrine of the Church."

4. QUESTION: **Are these warnings of the Pope justified by the experiences of the last forty years with the Soviet dictatorship?**

   ANSWER: They are. Whenever Soviet Power establishes itself, it not only betrays its promises of reform but turns these promises into their opposites.

5. QUESTION: **Can you give outstanding examples of this experience?**

   ANSWER: Yes, for there are many. Thus wherever the Soviet dictatorship sets itself up it abolishes free trade unions and does not permit collective bargaining or the right to strike. When it gets control of any colonial or colored people, as in China, its so-called "liberation" of them is actually the extention and intensification of slavery. From the time of Marx to Khrushchev, the Communist movement and Soviet Power have also carried forward and stimulated subtle and effective anti-Semitism.

6. QUESTION: **Has the trade union movement of this country recognized the hypocritical attitude of Soviet Communism toward the rights of the free trade unions?**

   ANSWER: Yes. On many occasions. Specifically, in September, 1959, the Executive Council of the AFL-CIO refused to meet with Dictator Khrushchev when he was on his mission to spread appeasement in the United States.

The overwhelming vote in favor of this rejection of any contact with Khrushchev was based on the fact that he represented a regime which suppressed the free trade unions.

7. QUESTION: **Can you cite one other striking illustration, from out of experiences in this country within trade unions, that justify this labor condemnation of the Soviet dictatorship?**

ANSWER: In 1950, this condemnation was brought out strikingly by several committees of the Congress of Industrial Organizations (then a separate body), when these committees presented reports on Red-ruled unions within the CIO. Each committee recommended the expulsion of these Red-ruled unions from the Congress of Industrial Organizations.

8. QUESTION: **What was the indictment against the Communists in their operations in the trade unions, which formed the heart of these reports?**

ANSWER: In each report, it was stated: "The committee finds that the fundamental purpose of the Communist Party is to promote the interests of the Soviet Union. It finds that, although the Communist Party has claimed to champion unionism and organization, it has always done so in order to carry on Communist work to pervert their policies to the advantage of the Soviet Union. The Communist Party, the committee finds, does not believe in trade unions. It believes in using trade unions. And it believes in using them for the purposes of the Soviet Union."

9. QUESTION:  **Is this Communist method of using reforms without actually believing in them a direct result of the Communist world view?**

   ANSWER:  It is. For under that view—as Lenin states in **State and Revolution**—no genuine freedom is possible until the Communist society has been won. Since this Communist society cannot be gained without the achievement of the dictatorship, according to Marxism-Leninism, all mass organizations are expendable in the struggle to set up the dictatorship. The trade unions, for example, are of no consequence in themselves; they are for the Communists merely convenient agencies to achieve the aims of the vanguard.

10. QUESTION:  **Has this concept of using reforms merely as a means to advance the Communist line and bring about the dictatorship been emphasized in any authoritative Red document?**

   ANSWER:  Outstanding in this respect, there is the great Communist guide book of theory and tactics written by Joseph Stalin. This contains one whole sub-section dealing with "Reformism and Revolutionism," contained in the **Foundations of Leninism.**

11. QUESTION:  **How does Stalin distinguish between the advocacy of reforms by a mere reformist and the same advocacy by a revolutionary or Communist?**

   ANSWER:  He shows very clearly from the Communist viewpoint that "to a reformist, reforms are everything." But the Communist "will accept a reform in order to use it as an aid in combining legal work with illegal work, to intensify under its cover, the illegal work for the revolutionary preparation of the masses for the overthrow of the bourgeoisie."

12. QUESTION: **What does this mean to us?**

ANSWER: It means that the Communists will seek to enter every movement in non-Soviet countries which aims at establishing the rights of the trade unions or Negro rights or oppose anti-Semitism. It means it will use this penetration and participation to induce certain thoughtless people to throw the mantle of protection around the Communist conspiracy here. The excuse will be that the Communists will stand for "progress," a word which the Reds frequently use.

13. QUESTION: **Was this misuse of reforms to advance the Communist cause presented to the comrades in the United States by any guide for infiltration?**

ANSWER: It was. This method of using reforms as a means to advance the Communist cause was recommended as a model for working secretly in all organizations by John Williamson, a member of the American Politburo, in the November, 1950, issue of **Political Affairs.**

14. QUESTION: **What is the "American Politburo" and what is "Political Affairs"?**

ANSWER: The "Politburo" is the governing agency of the Communist Party in the United States, modeled after the Politburo in Moscow, which is now known as the Praesidium. It is now known as the National Executive Committee, as the Communists frequently change the names of their organizational units to confuse American investigations and discussions.

**Political Affairs** is the official theoretical organ of the Communist Party, formerly known as **The Communist.**

15. QUESTION: **What is the concealed individual Communist (or the concealed Red cell) in an organization told by Williamson to do first of all?**

ANSWER: The individual concealed Communist (or the members of the Red cell) must look around for "immediate needs" upon which he can base agitation. He must seek out those grievances or arguments which will appeal to those around him as non-Communist in character; that is the meaning of "immediate needs" or "immediate demands."

16. QUESTION: **What is he supposed to do after he has raised these "immediate needs" as a base for getting action?**

ANSWER: According to Williamson and the Communist tactics at all times, the concealed Communist is obliged to link up these "immediate needs" with the line of the Party, with those things which the Kremlin wants done in America at that particular period.

17. QUESTION: **Whom is the concealed Communist supposed to persuade to forward the line of the Party in an organization which is being penetrated?**

ANSWER: He is supposed to persuade willing non-Communists to bring forward the line of the

Party, so that it will not be recognized generally as the Communist and so that the Communist himself will not be "exposed" as a Communist.

18. QUESTION: **By methods of this sort, have the Communists been able to penetrate originally non-Communist organizations and get them to advance the Communist line?**

ANSWER: Yes. This has been done in many cases. An outstanding illustration is the successful penetration of the Institute of Pacific Relations, which was used as the fulcrum to influence our State Department to betray the Chinese people into Red Chinese hands.

19. QUESTION: **How was this done?**

ANSWER: It was done by the Communists taking control of the executive staff, which in an organization like the Institute of Pacific Relations is the decisive agency. The busy industrialists, lawyers, and university presidents on the boards and committees were manipulated by the executive and technical staffs, which were loaded down with Communists or those under Communist influences.

20. QUESTION: **How did this whole maneuver in the IPR fit in with the use of reforms to advance the Communist line?**

ANSWER: Those wealthy and influential non-Communists who joined the IPR did so under the belief that they were forwarding good will among the nations in the Pacific and also helping to ameliorate the harsh conditions of colonial rule. Instead, as extensive hearings

by the Senate Sub-Committee on Internal
Security in the early 1950's showed, they
were being used to get our State Department and Government in general to assist in
the fastening of Red Chinese tyranny on the
mainland of China.

21. QUESTION: **Was enough public sentiment organized in
America by the Communists, favorable to
the false idea that the Reds stood for reforms
in themselves, to bring about other victories
for the Communist line?**

ANSWER: That by and large is the history of the last
twenty-five years. As outstanding examples
there was the American acquiescence in the
betrayal of all the nations now behind the
iron curtain into Soviet hands, at the end of
World War II.

There was also the "compelling" of the
United States to go to the summit conference
in Geneva in 1955. While we talked there
endlessly, Soviet Russia made its break-
through into the Middle East.

In like manner was the United States also
"forced" to go to Geneva in 1959 and to invite Dictator Nikita Khrushchev to our own
country in the same year.

Every one of these steps, and many more,
were hatched in Moscow, with instructions
given to support them to the Communists of
the eighty-three countries in which they
operate. Then, in time, the United States
bowed to Moscow's will in each case.

22. QUESTION: **Has a clear distinction been made between
reforms, including the right to organize and**

> the struggle against discrimination, and the Communist line?

ANSWER: There has, in the various Papal Encyclicals on the social question, including specifically **Quadragesimo Anno** and **Divini Redemptoris** by Pope Pius XI.

## REFERENCES AND SUGGESTED READINGS:

Reports and Hearings of the Senate Sub-Committee on Internal Security and House Committee on Un-American Activities, which deal with Communist penetration and Communist fronts. The student will have to write for those documents now available to: Research Department, Senate Sub-Committee on Internal Security, Senate Office Building, Washington, D.C. Also, to Francis E. Walter, Chairman, House Committee on Un-American Activities, House Office Building, Washington, D.C.

Above all: Consult Report by Senate Sub-Committee on Internal Security on the Institute of Pacific Relations, July 2, 1952.

The student can also write President George Meany, AFL-CIO, AFL Building, Washington, D.C., for copies of official labor reports dealing with the Communist menace to the unions.

CHAPTER V

# THE CATHOLIC CHURCH
# AND COMMUNISM

1. QUESTION: **Has the Catholic Church explained and re-futed the serious errors of Marxism?**

   ANSWER: Yes! Early and frequently. In 1846 Pius IX pronounced a solemn condemnation of "that infamous doctrine of so-called Communism, which is absolutely contrary to the natural law, and if once adopted would utterly destroy the rights, property and possessions of all men, and even Society itself." (This was two years before the **Communist Manifesto** was published.)

   In 1878 Pope Leo XIII defined Communism as: "The fatal plague which insinuates itself into the marrow of human society, only to bring about its ruin."

   The Supreme Pontiff Pius XI, prior to 1937, wrote nine official documents on the evils of Communism. On March 19th, 1937, his renowned Encyclical on "Atheistic Communism" was widely acclaimed in all free nations. It is an excellent summary of Marxism-Leninism.

2. QUESTION: **What did Pius XI say of this "Bolshevistic and Atheistic Communism?"**

   ANSWER: That "the all too imminent danger" of our own days is "Bolshevistic and Atheistic

Communism, which aims at upsetting the social order and at undermining the very foundations of Christian civilization."

3. QUESTION:   **How did Pius XI characterize this "Atheistic Communism?"**

ANSWER:   As a "satanic scourge," carrying on throughout the world "diabolical propaganda."

4. QUESTION:   **Upon what did Pius XI further say Communism builds its strength?**

ANSWER:   It "conceals in itself a false messianic idea" shot through "with a deceptive mysticism, which communicates a zealous and contagious enthusiasm to the multitudes entrapped by delusive promises."

(Of course, both this "false messianic idea" and "deceptive mysticism" arise from the two-fold false promises of Marxism-Leninism: A. That injustice to the workers shall be remedied when the "dictatorship of the proletariat" or socialism is established, and B. That when this dictatorship "withers away," it will be succeeded by the earthly paradise of the Communist society.)

5. QUESTION:   **Was the way prepared for Communism by preceding anti-religious doctrines?**

ANSWER:   Yes; Pius XI points out that in days past groups of "intellectuals" were formed "in an arrogant attempt to free civilization from the bonds of morality and religion." Always the preceding Popes had drawn the attention of the world to the subsequent "consequences of the de-Christianization of human society."

(These "philosophies" were also accompanied by such movements as Grand Orient Free Masonry and the Illuminati.)

6. QUESTION: **What further description of Communism is found in the 1937 Encyclical?**

   ANSWER: Its propaganda "so truly diabolical that the world perhaps never witnessed its like before" is directed "from one common center." Then we read: "It is shrewdly adapted to the varying conditions of diverse peoples. It has at its disposal great financial resources, gigantic organizations, international congresses, and countless trained workers. It makes use of pamphlets and reviews, of cinema, theatre and radio, of schools and even universities."

7. QUESTION: **How then does the Pope tell us it carries on its penetrations, forwarding what we have learned is "the Communist line?"**

   ANSWER: Here is the literal statement of Pius XI: "Little by little it penetrates into all classes of the people and even reaches the better-minded groups of the community, with the result that few are aware of the poison which increasingly pervades their minds and hearts."

8. QUESTION: **Does this mean, as the Pope puts it, that even believers in God, including Catholics, can sometimes be tricked into following the Communist line?**

   ANSWER: Most decidedly, and that is why Pius XI devoted a whole section of his encyclical to warning against the "trickery in various forms" used by the Communists. It was because of this that His Holiness warned, speaking to the Bishops: "See to it, Venerable Brethren, that the faithful do not allow themselves to be deceived! Communism is intrinsically wrong, and no one who would save Christian civilization may collaborate with it in any undertaking whatsoever."

9. QUESTION: **Why did Pius XI brand Communism as "intrinsically wrong" and a "satanic scourge?"**

ANSWER: Because Communism as a philosophy of life is evil in its very nature: always, everywhere, and in all its essential features.

10. QUESTION: **Why is Communism intrinsically evil?**

ANSWER: Because it is materialistic and atheistic. It is a denial of human spiritual dignity, human rights, and human freedom.

11. QUESTION: **Have "the great Communist scientists," Marx, Engels, Lenin and Stalin, acknowledged this fundamental materialistic (and therefore atheistic) character of Communism?**

ANSWER: Each one of them in turn has proclaimed materialism as the foundation stone of all the other Communist tenets. Thus, Frederick Engels in his work, **Ludwig Feuerbach,** makes the assault on all belief in God the very heart of that work. Thus V. I. Lenin in his booklet, **The Teachings of Karl Marx,** which is widely distributed by the Communists in America today, makes materialism and the materialistic conception of the world the basis for all of the Marxist ideas. And thus Joseph V. Stalin, in chapter 4 of his **History of the Communist Party of the Soviet Union,** states emphatically in a phrase often quoted by the Communists: "Dialectical materialism is the world outlook of the Marxist-Leninist Party."

12. QUESTION: **What attitude does this materialism lead the Communists to take in regard to religion?**

ANSWER: One of the utmost hostility, which leads to the determination to destroy religion, sometimes by weakening it through divisions and sometimes by stamping it out by force.

As Lenin says in vol. 11 of his **Selected Works** (page 664): "Religion is the opium of the people—this dictum of Marx's is the cornerstone of the whole Marxist view on religion. Marxism has always regarded all modern religions and churches and all religious organizations as instruments of bourgeois reaction that serve to defend exploitation and to drug the working class."

13. QUESTION: **Apart from Russia, have we any proof that Communism is a brutal system of inhuman cruelty, tyranny and religious hatred?**

ANSWER: Yes, we have many such proofs. That is the story in every country behind the iron curtain. It has been signalized in Soviet perfidy and brutality exhibited in the massacre of the Hungarian freedom fighters. It has been seen in the killing off of thousands in China, as lately as 1958, in the "rectification campaign." Against the Catholic Church, this has been evidenced in the enforced schism in China and in the taking over by Soviet Power of the apparatus of the Church in Hungary.

14. QUESTION: **Did Pius XI bring forward such proofs in his Encyclical?**

ANSWER: Yes. a) The horrible persecutions of Christians in Mexico in 1910 and after, where Catholic Churches were destroyed, priests arrested and put to death; the Catholic press was suppressed and violence tolerated. b) The Spanish Civil War in the early thirties: In this Soviet-sponsored revolution, planned for more than thirty years, with diabolic propaganda preceding, anti-clericism was featured and numerous conflicting political parties were organized by the International Conspirators. Several hundred Catholic Churches were destroyed; and thousands of Catholic priests, nuns, and social workers were killed. (Millions of non-combatants perished, but Spain was saved by the grace of God, by deep faith and heroic courage, under the leadership of Franco.)

15. QUESTION: **How did Pius XI explain the origin, success and popular appeal of a system which is intrinsically wrong?**

ANSWER: The saintly Pontiff advanced several basic reasons which are as valid today as they were 32 years ago. Namely: a) Every error seems to contain an element of truth; e.g., the Bolshevists stress the evils of private enterprise. b) Most persons are not aware of the insidious evils of Marxism. c) The young, especially, are not well informed about the satanic nature of Communism. d) The false intellectuals and liberals regarded Marxism as a new Socio-Economic System worthy of their support.

16. QUESTION: **What is the meaning, incidentally, of "Bolshevist" or "Bolshevik?"**

ANSWER: It means "a member of the majority," not alluding to the majority among the people. The Communists or Marxist-Leninist Party, as Lenin organized it on the basis of the Marxian ideas, must always be a small group imposing their will by guile and infiltration in the first place and then by force upon the people of any country. The word "majority," as used here, refers to the fact that the followers of V. I. Lenin received a majority vote on certain points in an important socialist convention in London, held some years before the Revolution in Russia.

17. QUESTION: **What part did Pius XI say "a large section of the non-Catholic press" played in the spread and success of Marxism-Leninism?**

ANSWER: On this important issue, the same illustrious Pontiff said: "A third powerful factor in the diffusion of Communism is the conspiracy of silence on the part of a large section of the non-Catholic press of the world." At that time, he pointed out that this "conspiracy" had been evidenced by: a) The failure of many papers to expose the horror perpetrated in Russia, in Mexico, and even in a great part of Spain; b) the failure of many to indict as they could "a world organization as vast as Russian Communism," upon whose repugnant aspects so many journals remained silent.

18. QUESTION: **Is this indictment by Pius XI of "a large section of the non-Catholic press" still applicable to many of our general or secular journals?**

ANSWER: Unfortunately, it is, even to the point where we seldom see any intelligent and popular indictment of the "Marxist-Leninist classics," which would enlighten the American people at once on the fact that the very nature of Communism makes it impossible for us to deal with it except for our ruination.

In addition, in many of our leading secular journals, we see no references to the publications from Moscow and Peking, sent to the Communists here steadily, and an examination of which would alert the American people in advance to the Communist line.

19. QUESTION: **Did the Government of the United States help the cause of Communism in Spain and elsewhere at this time (1932-1937)?**

ANSWER: Decidedly. It allowed the "Abraham Lincoln Brigade" openly and illegally to recruit American soldiers for service in the Loyalist (i.e. Marxist) army. It encouraged reds, pinkos and fellow-travellers to circulate widely their misleading propaganda and to attack publicly General Franco and the defenders of religious and civic freedom in Spain.

20. QUESTION: **Did the Government of the United States also help to build up Soviet Communist rule**

over other places by its policies of appeasement?

ANSWER: Yes. As has been previously indicated, from 1933 on, the Government of the United States, with the exception of the few years of the Hitler-Stalin Pact (1939-1941) has acquiesced in the brutal establishment of Soviet rule over every country now behind the Iron Curtain.

21. QUESTION: **What did Pius XI recommend to the Catholic press by way of advancing social study and offsetting Communism?**

ANSWER: He strongly advised the Catholic press to play a prominent part in the following moves: a) "to foster in various attractive ways an ever better understanding of social doctrine," which of course meant engaging in the championship of social reform of a sound character for the working classes; b) to supply "accurate and complete information on the activity of the (Communist) enemy and the means of resistance found most effective in various quarters;" and c) to "warn against the insidious deceits with which Communists endeavor all too successfully to attract even men of good faith."

(It can be seen that Pius XI is urging here a particular crusade of enlightenment in the Catholic press on the Communist line.)

22. QUESTION: **Did Pius XI counsel positive action for Christian charity and social justice in addition to recommending intelligent and vigilant action against Communism as it actually operates?**

ANSWER: Most emphatically. In turn and at some
length, he emphasized: a) The renewal of
Christian life as the basis for all social
reform and as answering the atheism of
Communism; b) the pursuit of Christian
charity, which would not only include helping those who are in difficulties but also in
leading "a more moderate way of life;"
c) the strict following out of Christian social
justice, as stressed so definitely in Pius XI's
Encyclical **Quadragesimo Anno,** to which he
referred again, and also in Leo XIII's **Rerum
Novarum** (On the Condition of Labor).

23. QUESTION: **In connection with this emphasis on social
justice, did Pius XI mention specifically the
rights of the labor movement and the deplorable acts of "those Catholic industrialists" who try to block the right to organize?**

ANSWER: Yes, he singled out for criticism "certain
Catholic circles" who have "refused to understand that Christian charity demands the
recognition of certain rights due to the
working man, which the Church has explic-
itly acknowledged." And His Holiness continued: "Is it not deplorable that the right of
private property defended by the Church
should so often have been used as a weapon
to defraud the working man of his just
salary and his social rights?"

24. QUESTION: **How did Catholics, generally, react to the
Papal teaching on Communism?**

ANSWER: The majority of Catholics throughout the
world accepted these truths on Atheistic

Communism (Marxism-Leninism), gratefully and with great concern. But millions of devout Catholics soon forgot the essentials of the Encyclical and failed to seek further knowledge about it. Many did not study the Encyclical, and the other pronouncements of the Papacy on social questions, in order to put them into action. In a word, they did not examine them and learn from them to the same extent that the Communists learned from the "Marxist-Leninist classics"—the teachings of Marx, Engels, Lenin, Stalin, Mao Tse-tung, and now Khrushchev.

25. QUESTION: **Did Pius XI recommend the study of social problems as enunciated by the Papal Encyclicals?**

ANSWER: That is one of the chief features of Pius XI's counsels: The promotion of "a wider study of social problems in the light of the doctrine of the Church." This social study and propaganda were urged for two chief reasons: a) To disseminate widely the social teachings of the Church in a positive sense (such as the right to organize, championship of the just rights of the Negro people, Christian opposition to anti-Semitism, legislation favorable to the just claims of the working classes), and b) to understand the nature, the tactics, and the trickery of the Communist enemy.

26. QUESTION: **What is one of the great dangers for the Catholics in America that we can learn from these counsels and repeated warnings of Pius XI?**